Enjoy this walk, and may the sun shine all day, your boots feel comfortable on your feet and your pack feels as light as a feather! Happy walking! John N. Merrill

Something to ponder.

As we walk around this amazing world, we take for granted the stunning diversity of life and nature. We pass the slopes of mountains and the river valleys. We see birds, insects, animals and all the kaleidoscope of flowers and trees. But let's stop for a moment and just stand in awe of this plethora of sights. However hard we, as humans try, we cannot match the magnificence that our eyes see. Whether you are spiritual or not, you cannot ignore or be moved to wonder at the incredible work of a higher dimension - the divine.

While many would say this is evolution, there still has be "someone", who first thought up the flower, tree, bird, animal, and landscape. You only have to gaze at a small mountain flower and see the delicate stems and petals made to perfection. Whilst the earth's movement have created our landscape, the forces of the divine have been at work to help create that breathtaking view. We on the other-hand have been given eyes and feelings, so that we can appreciate and stand in awe at the sight before us.

So as we wander down a path in woodland or high mountains, where the whole spectrum of life is laid out for us to see. Lets give eternal thanks for being able to walk and see these things first hand. To be able to touch, feel and appreciate the work of the divine, makes the effort more than worthwhile. So, as you walk, stop and ponder at the never ending variety of sights and smells that confront us on each stride we take.

John N. Merrill 2014

Illustrated Talks
by Revd. John N. Merrill

*John has countless talks on his recording breaking walks around the world.
For a full list contact John - Tel. 01992-762776
Email - marathonhiker@aol.com*

His latest talks -

WALKING TO MONT ST. MICHEL - John has walked here twice - from Farnham via Winchester to Mont St. Michel (200 miles), and from Caen (100 miles) joining the annual pilgrimage walk organised by the Association of Chemins de Mont St. Michel. Both remarkable walks with the final 7km across the exposed sand, mud and rivers to the rock and abbey.

LONDON TO OXFORD PILGRIMAGE WALK - St. Frideswide Way - 93 miles. John discovers and traces the medieval pilgrimage route from Westminster Abbey to Christ Church Cathedral in Oxford, and the shrine of St. Frideswide. Then onto Binsey and her "forgotten" healing well; the Lourdes of the South.

WALKING ESSEX'S COASTLINE - 250 MILES - An exceptional walk around England's second largest county's coastline, rich in history, sea-birds and waders and more than 100 islands. A surprising journey.

WALKING MY WAY - The on going story of John's unique walking life, with some 219,000 miles walked. The stories and tales from his ground breaking walks around the world.

OTHER JOHN MERRILL DAY CHALLENGE WALKS -

WHITE PEAK CHALLENGE WALK
THE HAPPY HIKER - WHITE PEAK - CHALLENGE WALK No.2
DARK PEAK CHALLENGE WALK
PEAK DISTRICT END TO END WALKS
STAFFORDSHIRE MOORLANDS CHALLENGE WALK
THE LITTLE JOHN CHALLENGE WALK
YORKSHIRE DALES CHALLENGE WALK
NORTH YORKSHIRE MOORS CHALLENGE WALK
LAKELAND CHALLENGE WALK
THE RUTLAND WATER CHALLENGE WALK
MALVERN HILLS CHALLENGE WALK
THE SALTER'S WAY
THE SNOWDON CHALLENGE
CHARNWOOD FOREST CHALLENGE WALK
THREE COUNTIES CHALLENGE WALK (Peak District).
CAL-DER-WENT WALK
THE QUANTOCK WAY
BELVOIR WITCHES CHALLENGE WALK
THE CARNEDDAU CHALLENGE WALK
THE SWEET PEA CHALLENGE WALK
THE LINCOLNSHIRE WOLDS - BLACK DEATH - CHALLENGE WALK
JENNIFER'S CHALLENGE WALK
THE EPPING FOREST CHALLENGE WALK
THE THREE BOROUGH CHALLENGE WALK - NORTH LONDON
THE HERTFORD CHALLENGE WALK
THE BOSHAM CHALLENGE WALK
NORFOLK BROADS CHALLENGE WALK
THE KING JOHN CHALLENGE WALK
THE SURREY HILLS CHALLENGE WALK
THE RIVER MIMRAM CHALLENGE WALK
THE BRIGHTON WAY
THE ISLE OF THANET CHALLENGE WALK
THE RIVER WEY & GODALMING NAVIGATIONS
EAST DEVON CHALLENGE WALK

THE
BRIGHTON
WAY

by Revd. John N. Merrill

THE JOHN MERRILL FOUNDATION
32, Holmesdale, Waltham Cross, Hertfordshire, England. EN8 8QY

Tel/Fax - 01992-762776
E-mail - john@johnmerrillwalkguides.co.uk
www.johnmerrillwalkguides.co.uk
www.thejohnmerrillministry.co.uk
www.londoninterfaithchurch.co.uk

A catalogue record for this book is available from the British Library.

Conceived, edited, typset and designed by *The John Merrill Foundation*
Printed and handmade by *John N. Merrill.*
Book layout and cover design by *John N. Merrill*

© Text and photographs - by Revd. John N. Merrill 2013
© Maps by Revd. John N. Merrill, HonMUniv, R.I.M.A. 2013
© Additional material - Revd. John N. Merrill, HonMUniv, 2013.

ISBN 978 - 0-9574186-6-0
First Published - January 2013. Revised and reprinted - May 2013.
Special limited edition.

Typeset in Humanst521 - bold, italic, and plain 11pt, 14pt and 18pt
Main titles in 18pt .**Humanst521 Bd BT** by John Merrill in Adobe Pagemaker on a iMac.

Please note - *The maps in this guide are purely illustrative. You are encouraged to use the appropriate 1:25,000 O.S. Explorer map as detailed on each walk.*

John Merrill confirms he has walked all the routes in this book and detailed what he found. Meticulous research has been undertaken to ensure that this publication is highly accurate at the time of going to press. The publishers, however, cannot be held responsible for alterations, errors, omissions, or for changes in details given. They would welcome information to help keep the book up to date.

Cover design & photo's © The John Merrill Foundation 2013.
Photographs by Revd. John N. Merrill.

The John Merrill Foundation maintains the John Merrill Library and archives and administers the worldwide pubishing rights of John Merrill's works in all media formats.

Printed on paper from a 100% sustainable forest.
The John Merrill Foundation plants sufficient trees through the
Woodland Trust to replenish the trees used in its publications.

CONTENTS

The author outside Chartres Cathedral, France, after walking there from Paris. August 2017.

A little about Revd. John N. Merrill

John is unique, possessing the skills of a marathon runner, mountain climber and athlete. Since his first 1,000 mile walk through the islands of the Inner and Outer Hebrides in 1970, he has since walked over 219,000 miles and worn out 133 pairs of boots, 49 rucksacks and more than 1,600 pairs of socks. He has brought marathon walking to Olympic standard. He has done a 1,000 mile walk through the Orkneys and Shetlands and a 1,600 mile walk up the length of of the west coast of Ireland. In 1978 he became the first person to walk around the entire coastline of Britain - 7,000 miles. He has walked across Europe, the Alps and Pyrenees - 3,000 miles with 600,000 feet of ascent and descent. In America he has walked the 2,500 mile Appalachian Trail; the Pacific Crest Trail - 2,500 miles in record time; the Continental Divide Trail; became the first person to thru-hike the Buckeye Trail - 1,350 miles in Ohio and completed a unique 4,260 mile walk in 178 days coast to coast across America. He has climbed all the mountains in New Mexico and walked all the trails.

In Britain he has walked all the National Trails many times; linked all the National Parks and trails in a 2,060 mile walk; completed a 1,608 mile Land's End to John o' Groats walk and countless other unique walks. He has walked three times to Santiago de Compostella (Spain) via different routes; to St. Olav's Shrine in Norway - 420 miles; walked to Assisi, St. Gilles du Gard, the Cathar Ways and to Mont St. Michel. He has walked every long distance path in France and Germany, and walked to every pilgrimage destination in England and France, and extensively walked in every country in Europe.

He has walked in Africa; all the trails in the Hong Kong Islands; and completed five trekking expeditions to the Himalyas and India. Not only is he the world's leading marathon walker he is Britain's most experienced walker. John is author of more than 440 walk guides which have sold more than 4 million copies with more than 1 million sold on the Peak District alone. He has created more than 80 challenge walks which have been used to raise, so far, more than a £1 million for different charities.

John has never broken a bone or been lost and never had any trouble anywhere. He still walks in the same body he was born with, has had no replacements and does not use poles. This he puts down to his deep spiritual nature and in 2010 he was ordained as a multi-faith Minister - a universal monk, *"honouring and embracing all faiths and none"*. He conducts weddings and funerals, teaches Qigong and is a Reiki practioner. He gives talks all over the UK.

INTRODUCTION

I am indebted to Norman Willis whose book I subsequently published on this walk in 2002. He created the route after many years of travelling by train along the route and kept wanting to explore the area on foot. Seeing the book needed updating and being on my doorstep I felt I should walk the route and upgrade the maps I did and rewrite the book; so I dedicate this book to him.

Being December and short daylight hours I took four days over the walk - 12 to 17 miles a day, as I "Stationed hopped" to Brighton. It is a lovely walk from the flight path of Gatwick airport, through gentle countryside, where sheep roam and much woodland. The villages were full of history and several with amazing churches were passed. But the glory of the walk is after Hassocks Station where you reach the South Downs and windmills. The downs reminded me of the dales of the Peak District, although more expansive and where sheep roamed. A gentle ascent brings into their domain with extensive views - all worth the 40 miles of walking to get here. You cross the downs following a section of the South Downs Way, with panoramic views and to the sea. Eventually you cross your last hill and descend to the pebbled shore and onto Brighton Pier and Station. A delightful walk that has it all - famous graves, deer, woodland, towns and villages, sweeping gentle hills and rolling waves. There is sprinkling of inns at the end of each section, but most of the time you will have to carry what you need.

Enjoy the walk, leaving the frantic world of transport and communication behind as you walk southwards through Sussex to the glimmering sea. Forget your problems and timetables, just enjoy Mother Earth and the beauty of the landscape and the sound of sheep and birds. A regular dose of this enriches your life immeasurably and you realise nothing is important.

Enjoy your walk to the sea!

Happy walking!
John N. Merrill

HOW TO DO IT

The whole walk is covered by the following 1:25,000 Explorer Ordnance Survey Maps - in walking order -

> *146 - Dorking, Box Hill & Reigate.*
> *134 - Crawley & Billingshurst.*
> *135 - Ashdown Forest.*
> *122 - Brighton & Hove.*

The walk starts at Horley Station on the London to Brighton line and links the following stations together -

Horley, Three Bridges, Balcombe, Haywards Heath, Wivelsfield, Hassocks, Falmer and Brighton. The only exception is Falmer which is on the Brighton - Eastbourne line.

There is no timetable to do the walk in, just do it at your own pace. It is a challenge to walk it all in a day; two days is also challenging at over 25 miles per day. A three day schedule of about 17 miles a day allows time to explore the paces passed on the way. I did it over 3 1/2 days because I was restricted to the short daylight hours in December, time to photograph and make notes and travelling to and from London each day. You can do the walk over several days by using the stations as your end point and returning again the next day or weekend to continue.

The whole route is 53 1/2 miles long which includes the path links to some of the stations which you walk twice if "station hopping". If walking direct the distance from Horley to Brighton Station is 52 miles. I took 110,700 steps along the route - you basically average 2,000 steps a mile. I also burnt off some 800 calories for every 10 miles walked!

The stations and towns have inns, shops and cafe's but in-between there is nothing, so carry what you need. Brighton has everything at the end. There is little accommodation along the way, only at some of the inns close some of the stations - google for details.

Enjoy the walk and for the successful an embroidered badge and certificate are available from The John Merrill Foundation - see details at the rear of book.

ABOUT THE WALK
- some general comments.

Whilst every care is taken detailing and describing the walks in this book, it should be borne in mind that the countryside changes by the seasons and the work of man. I have described the walk to the best of my ability, detailing what I have found actually on the walk in the way of stiles and signs. You should always walk with the appropriate O.S. map, as detailed for each walk, open on the walk area for constant reference. Obviously with the passage of time stiles become broken or replaced by a ladder stile , a small gate or a kissing gate. Signs too have a habit of being broken or pushed over - vandalism. All the route follow rights of way and only on rare occasions will you have to overcome obstacles in its path, such as a blown down tree, barbed wire fence or an electric fence. On rare occasions rights of way are rerouted and these amendments are included in the next edition. Inns have a frustrating habit of changing their name, then back to the original one!

All rights of way have colour coded arrows; on marker posts, stiles/gates and trees; these help you to show the direction of the right of way -

Yellow - Public footpath.
Blue - Public bridleway.
Red - Byway open to all traffic (BOAT).
Black - Road used as a public path (RUPP).
White - Concessionary and Permissive path

The seasons bring occasional problems whilst out walking which should also be borne in mind. In the height of summer paths become overgrown and you may have to fight your way through in a few places. In low lying areas the fields are often full of crops, and although the pathline goes straight across it may be more practical to walk round the field edge to get to the next stile or gate. In summer the ground is generally dry but in autumn and winter, especially because of our climate, the surface can be decidedly wet and slippery; sometimes even gluttonous mud!

These comments are part of countryside walking which help to make your walk more interesting or briefly frustrating. Standing in a track up to your ankles in mud might not be funny at the time but upon reflection was one of the highlights of the walk!

The mileage for each section is based on three calculations -

1. pedometer and stepometer readings.
2. the route map measured on the map.
3. the time I took for the walk.

I believe the figure stated for each section to be very accurate but we all walk differently and not always in a straight line! The time allowed for each section is on the generous side and does not include pub stops etc. The figure is based on the fact that on average a person walks 2 1/2 miles an hours but less in hilly terrain. Allow 20 minutes to walk a mile; ten minutes for 1/2 mile and five minutes for 1/4 mile. On average you will walk 2,000 strides to a mile - an average stride is 31 inches..

"For every mile you walk, you extend your life by 21 minutes"

EQUIPMENT NOTES

Today there is a bewildering variety of walking gear, much is superfluous to general walking in Britain. As a basic observation, people over dress for the outdoors. Basically equipment should be serviceable and do the task. I don't use walking poles; humans were built to walk with two legs! The following are some of my thoughts gathered from my walking experiences.

BOOTS - For summer use and day walking I wear lightweight boots. For high mountains and longer trips I prefer a good quality boot with a full leather upper, of medium weight, traditional style ,with a vibram sole. I always add a foam cushioned insole to help cushion the base of my feet.

SOCKS - I generally wear two thick pairs as this helps minimise blisters. The inner pair are of loop stitch variety and approximately 80% wool. The outer are also a thick pair of approximately 80% wool. I often wear double inner socks, which minimise blisters.

CLOTHES & WATERPROOFS - for general walking I wear a T shirt or cotton shirt with a cotton wind jacket on top, and shorts - even in snow! You generate heat as you walk and I prefer to layer my clothes to avoid getting too hot. Depending on the season will dictate how many layers you wear. In soft rain I just use my wind jacket for I know it quickly dries out. In heavy or consistent rain I slip on a poncho, which covers me and my pack and allows air to circulate, while keeping me dry. Only in extreme conditions will I don over-trousers, much preferring to get wet and feel comfortable. I never wear gaiters, except when cross country skiing, or in snow and glacier crossings. I find running shorts and sleeveless T shirts ideal for summer.

FOOD - as I walk I carry bars of chocolate, for they provide instant energy and are light to carry. In winter a flask of hot coffee is welcome. I never carry water and find no hardship from not doing so, but this is a personal matter! From experience I find the more I drink the more I want and sweat. You should always carry some extra food such as trail mix & candy bars etc., for emergencies. Full milk is a very underestimated source of food and liquid.

RUCKSACKS - for day walking I use a rucksack of about 30/40 litre capacity and although it leaves excess space it does mean that the sac is well padded, with an internal frame and padded shoulder straps, chest strap and waist strap. Inside apart from the basics for one day, in winter I carry gloves, wear a hat/cap and carry a spare pullover and a pair of socks.

MAP & COMPASS - when I am walking I always have the relevant map - preferably 1:25,000 scale - open in my hand. This enables me to constantly check that I am walking the right way. In case of bad weather I carry a compass, which once mastered gives you complete confidence in thick cloud or mist - you should always know where you are; I have a built in direction finder! Map reading and compass work is a skill and should be learnt. With modern technology you can now downloaded OS maps to your phone, record your walk, mileage, calories, steps taken, walking speed and time taken.

THE ART OF WALKING THE JOHN MERRILL WAY

1. Always set off in the clothes you plan to wear all day, given the weather conditions. Only on sudden changes in the weather will I stop and put on a waterproof or warmer clothing.

2. Set off at a steady comfortable pace, which you can maintain all day. You should end the walk as fresh as when as you started.

3. Maintain your pace and don t stop. Stopping for any period of time disrupts your rhythm and takes upwards of a mile to settle back down into the flow/ease of movement.

4. Switch off your mobile phone and music centre, and listen and enjoy the countryside - the smells of the flowers, bird song, the rustle of the leaves and the tinkling stream.

5. Ignore the mileage and ascents - don t tick off the miles, just concentrate on what the walk s goal is. To think otherwise slows you down and makes the walk a struggle rather than a joy. In a similar vein, when ascending just keep a steady pace and keep going. To stop is to disrupt the flow and make the ascent interminable.

6. Whilst a walk is a challenge to complete, it is not just exercise. You should enjoy the world around you; the flowers, birds, wildlife and nature and look at and explore the historical buildings and church s that you pass. All are part of life s rich tapestry.

7. Remember that for every mile that you walk, you extend your life by 21 minutes.

8. A journey of a 1,000 miles begins with a single step and a mile requires 2,000 strides.

The expert traveller
leaves no footprints.
Lao Tzu.

FOLLOW THE COUNTRY CODE

* Be safe - plan ahead and follow any signs.

* Leave gates and property
as you find them.

* Protect plants and animals, and take
your litter home.

* Keep dogs
under close control.

* Consider
other people.

* Take only photographs,
leave only footprints.

OBSERVE THE HIKER'S CODE

* Hike only along marked routes - do not leave the trail.

* Use stiles to climb fences; close gates.

* Camp only in designated campsites.

* Carry a light-weight stove.

* Leave the trail cleaner than you found it.

* Leave flowers and plants for others to enjoy.

* Keep dogs on a leash.

* Protect and do not disturb wildlife.

* Use the trail at your own risk.

* Leave only your thanks and footprints - take nothing but photographs.

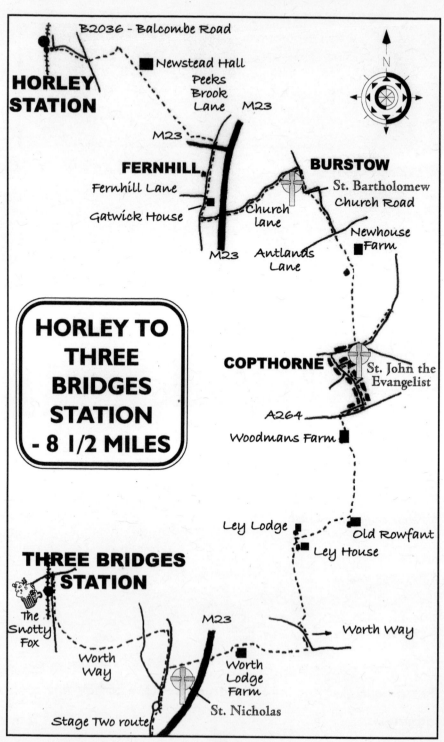

B2036 - Balcombe Road

Newstead Hall

Peeks Brook Lane

M23

HORLEY STATION

M23

FERNHILL

Fernhill Lane

Gatwick House

Church lane

M23

Antlands Lane

BURSTOW

St. Bartholomew Church Road

Newhouse Farm

HORLEY TO THREE BRIDGES STATION - 8 1/2 MILES

COPTHORNE

St. John the Evangelist

A264

Woodmans Farm

Ley Lodge

Old Rowfant

Ley House

THREE BRIDGES STATION

The Snotty Fox

Worth Way

M23

Worth Way

Worth Lodge Farm

St. Nicholas

Stage Two route

Section One

Horley Station to
Three Bridges Station. - 8 1/2 miles
18,118 steps - allow 3 to 4 hours.

Three Bridges Station

Basic route - Horley Station - B2036 (Balcombe Road) - Newstead Hall - Peeks Brook Lane - Fernhill - Church Lane - Burstow - Church Road - Newhouse Farm - Copthorne - St. Bartholomew Church - A264 - Woodmans Farm - Ley Lodge - Ley House - Worth Way - St. Nicholas Church, Worth - Worth Way - Three Bridges Station.

Maps- Ordnance Survey 1:25,000 Explorer Series Nos. - .
- 146 - Dorking, Box Hill & Reigate.
- 134 - Crawley & Billingshurst.
- 135 - Ashdown Forest.

Start - Horley Station Car park - NCP park at the side of the station on a lower level in The Drive. Map 146 - G.R. 286426.

Inns - Nothing until Three Bridges Station with The Snotty Fox opposite.

ABOUT THE STAGE - Basically well defined paths through flat countryside. At first the planes descending to nearby Gatwick Airport provide the background noise, before the countryside noise of birds and cattle are heard. You pass three interesting churches which, if time permits, are well worth exploring; all are very different. The final mile is along the Worth Way; part of which can be omitted is continuing on to Balcombe. There is an inn at the end, so carry all you need; you pass close to a shop in Copthorne, near The Green, approximately halfway.

WALKING INSTRUCTIONS - From the entrance of Horley Station, turn right along Victoria Road to the roundabout and junction with the B2036 - Balcombe Road. Cross on the right and turn left and a few meters later before house No. 137 - Edgewood, turn left, as footpath signed . Follow the tree lined path between the house gardens to the junction with the Millennium Trail.

MILLENNIUM TRAIL - (Reigate and Banstead Millennium Trail) - 18 miles (29 km). Runs from Riverside Gardens Park, Horley to Banstead Common, Banstead, Surrey.

Cross two bridges - one wooden and one stone - and turn right to a kissing gate. Continue on the path through a wood, still on the Millennium Trail. Pass Newstead Hall on your left and cross a lane. Continue ahead via a kissing gate, following the fenced path. The Millennium Trail, later turns right but you keep straight ahead for 1/4 mile to the junction with the Sussex Border Path.

SUSSEX BORDER PATH - Long distance path of some 150 miles close to the inland boundary of East and West Sussex. Created in 1983.
www.sussexborderpath.co.uk

Turn left, as path signed - Peeks Brook Lane 1/4 mile. Gaining the lane turn right, passing under the M23 and into the hamlet of Fernhill. Pass the Royal Oak House, on the right, and later Gatwick House on the left as the lane does a small Z bend. Immediately after turn left along Church Lane - Bridlepath signed. You basically keep straight ahead along it for little over 1/2 mile. First it is a road as you cross the bridge over the M23. The becomes a potholed track. After passing the house, Willows End on the left, you cross a small river bridge, as you follow a path; later there is evidence of the former tarmaced Church Lane. Reaching a road turn right into the hamlet of Burstow, passing Burstow Court on the right and now following a section of the Tandridge Border path. Soon pass Burstow Church dedicated to St. Bartholomew on the right. On the left is the Sunday School.

ST BARTHOLOMEW CHURCH - *As you enter the churchyard on your left is a small tombstone to - Albert Edward Leppard (1866 - 1917) - A true lover of nature. The church dates from 1121 and has a late mediaeval wooden tower. In the chancel is the plaque to John Flamstead (1646 - 1719), the first Astronomer Royal who was also Rector of Burstow from 1684 until his death in 1719. The Sunday School, opposite the church, has a plaque recording that it was built in 1859 from the proceeds of a bazaar, held in Burstow Hall on August 3rd. 1859.*

Where the road turns sharp left, cross to a stile on your right and onto another stile on your left. Cross the field to the far righthand corner and stile before Church Road; you are still on the Sussex Border path. Turn right along the road to the junction with Antlands Lane. Go straight across along the farm drive to Newhouse Farm - footpath signed. Pass a house on the right and at the farm go through a gate on the right of the drive. Follow the faint path, bearing slightly right, across the centre of the field, aiming for the furthest righthand corner of the field and a gate. Bear slightly left keeping the hedge on your left as you can see ahead the steeple of Copthorne church - your destination! Reach the edge of the village at a kissing gate and keep ahead on the road past houses to the main road, with the Pharmacy on the right and St. John's Cottage opposite.

Cross the road and turn left and then right and right again into Church Road and soon on your right is St. John the Evangelist church.

ST. JOHN THE EVANGELIST CHURCH - *Anglican built in 1885. Behind the church is a labyrinth with a sculpture in the middle - "Please pray for those remains are here interred."*
www.copthornechurch.org

Continue along Church Road and cross to your left, as path signed, to follow the tarmaced path along the lefthand side of the Green - to your right is the local shop. At the end of the path turn left along Newtown to Copthorne Common Road, immediately before the A264 road. Turn right along the No Through Road to its end, via short path to the A261 road. Cross with care to the concrete drive, opposite, and path sign. Follow the drive to Woodmans Farm and just afterwards where it goes to Coombs Wood Farm, continue ahead on a path, path signed. Walk through woodland and across a footbridge. Continue straight ahead on the path before a building ahead - Old Rowlant. Turn right, as path signed along a track passing a mill pond on the left and Lake Cottage and Mill Studio on the right. The track now becomes a road and shortly afterwards reach Ley Lodge on your right.

Turn left, as path signed, along the drive to Ley House. Turn right and left past the house, now on a track to a field and path sign. Continue ahead now following a path with a hedge on your left and a fence on the right. The path becomes a grass track to two stiles. Ascend gently with Leyhouse Wood on the left, as the path turns right to a road. To your left is Woodpeckers Fishery. Turn left along the main road, along its grassy verge on the right for a short distance before joining the tarmaced path of Worth Way.

WORTH WAY - Former railway line between East Grinstead and Three Bridges. Approx. 7 miles (11 km) long.

Soon afterwards the road turns sharp left and here as signed - Work Way - Worth 1 mile - turn right along the track. This leads around Worth Lodge Farm and over the M23 in 1/2 mile. Keep ahead and soon pass Worth Church to your left.

St. NICHOLAS CHURCH, WORTH - Dedicated to S. Nicholas. The most complete Saxon church in England, cruciform shape, with the string courses clearly visible. The Saxon chancel arch at 22 feet high is one of the largest in the country. The tower, by Anthony Salvin, was built in 1871.

Keep ahead along the road from the church to Church Road. Those not going to Three Bridges Station turn left here to continue along Stage Two. Turn right along the road for 1/4 mile to the house Fircroft and turn left, still following Worth Way. Follow the path and later turn right, as Three Bridges Stationed signed - and left to pass through a tunnel. Now along the former railway line follow it as it curves right to the main road more than 1/2 mile ahead. Turn right along Station Hill and descend gently to the A2220 and turn left. Pass under the railway bridge and left again to Three Bridges Station; opposite is the Snotty Fox Inn

17

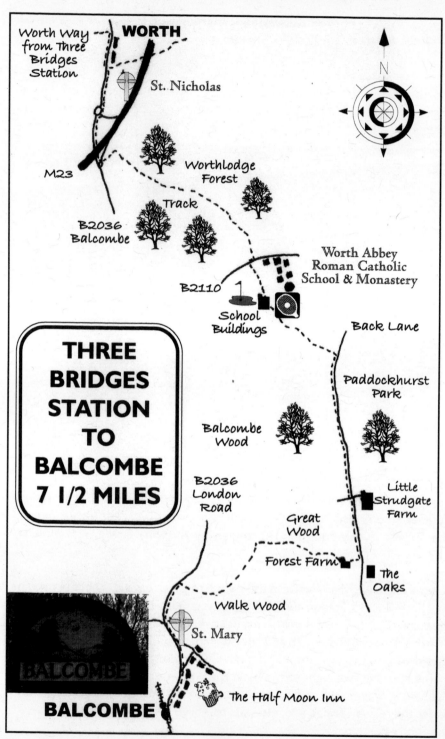

Worth Way from Three Bridges Station

WORTH

St. Nicholas

M23

Worthlodge Forest

Track

B2036 Balcombe

Worth Abbey Roman Catholic School & Monastery

B2110

School Buildings

Back Lane

Paddockhurst Park

THREE BRIDGES STATION TO BALCOMBE 7 1/2 MILES

Balcombe Wood

B2036 London Road

Little Strudgate Farm

Great Wood

Forest Farm

The Oaks

Walk Wood

St. Mary

BALCOMBE

BALCOMBE

The Half Moon Inn

N

Stage Two

Three Bridges Station to Balcombe Station
- 7 1/2 miles.
- allow 2 1/2 hours
- 15,220 steps

Basic Route - Three Bridges Station - Worth Way - Church Road - Balcombe Road - M23 -Worthlodge Forest - B2110 - Worth Abbey - Back Lane - Paddockhurst Park - Little Strudgate Farm - Forest Farm - Upperstaff Wood - B2036 (London Road) - St. Mary's Church, Salcombe - Salcombe Station.

Maps - Ordnance Survey Explorer Series Nos.
- 134 - Crawley & Horsham.
-135 - Ashdown Forest.

Start - Three Bridges Station & car park - GR 288369. Church Road, Worth for 'thru' hikers.

Inns - The Half Moon Inn in Balcombe 1/2 from Balcombe Station.

ABOUT THE WALK - Much of the route is along good paths through attractive woodland and forest. You pass Worth Abbey and near the end pass Balcombe church where the Shakespearean actor, Paul Schofield is buried

WALKING INSTRUCTIONS - From Three Bridges Station, turn right under the railway bridge and right again "up" Station Hill to where the Worth Way starts on your left (basically you are retracing your steps along the final mile of Stage One). Walk through the tunnel and then ascend and turn left, to continue along the signed Worth Way to Church Road, opposite Fircroft. Turn right and at the junction to Worth church keep straight ahead on the left along the tarmaced path. Thru hikers follow this path.

Descend to a roundabout and the B2036 road - Balcombe Road. Cross to the right and keep ahead following the Balcombe road to another roundabout, with the slip road on the left, from the M23. Cross to the left and across the top of the slip road to a path sign. Follow the defined path soon ascending through Worthlodge Forest on a defined track. The path is well signed and you basically keep straight ahead. In 3/4 mile follow track right and left, as signed, continuing ahead to the B2110 road 1/4 mile away. Just to your left is the entrance gatehouse to Worth Abbey.

The track in Worthlodge Forest.

WORTH ABBEY - Benedictine Monastery with 25 Roman Catholic monks. Founded in 1933 by monks from Downside Abbey, Somerset. The impressive circular church and Abbey Shop are open daily.
www.worthabbey.net

Turn right and left to a path sign and keep the fence and later wall of Worth Abbey grounds on your left with a golf course on your right. Reach a kissing gate and keep ahead along the paved drive past school buildings to tennis courts on your left. Keep ahead now on a track as you descend to a bridge. Ascend the path beyond beside Downside Wood, on your left, to Back Lane - 3/4 mile from the B2110 & Worth Abbey, and spot height 129 metres. Turn right and follow the quiet wooded lane for 1 1/4 miles. In less a mile reach a road junction with Little Strudgate Farm on the left with the farm road to Great Strudgate Farm. Keep ahead, now along Paddockhurst Lane and take the third right of way on your right. Pass two on the right then Square Wood on the left and before The Oaks, turn right, as path signed, along the track past Forest Farm. Keep ahead and descend to a stile. Keep ahead to another and edge of Upperstaff Wood. As path signed turn half right across the field to a path sign over the brow to the edge of Great Wood. As path signed, bear left and soon right into woodland and cross a long wooden "bridge". Keep ahead to a track junction. Turn left and follow the wide track past woodland - Walk Wood on the left, to the Balcombe Road, B2036, little over 1/2 mile away.

Turn left along the tarmaced path and soon reach Balcombe church on the left.

ST. MARY'S CHURCH, BALCOMBE - *An earlier church occupied the site in the late 11th. century. The present church dates back to the 13th. century with the tower built in the 15th. century. Paul Scofield, the actor of both stage and screen, who lived in the village all his life, is buried here* www.stmarys-balcombe. org

Keep left then right, following London Road, through Balcombe straight to Balcombe Station. The Half Moon Inn is along the road to your left as you walk through Balcombe.

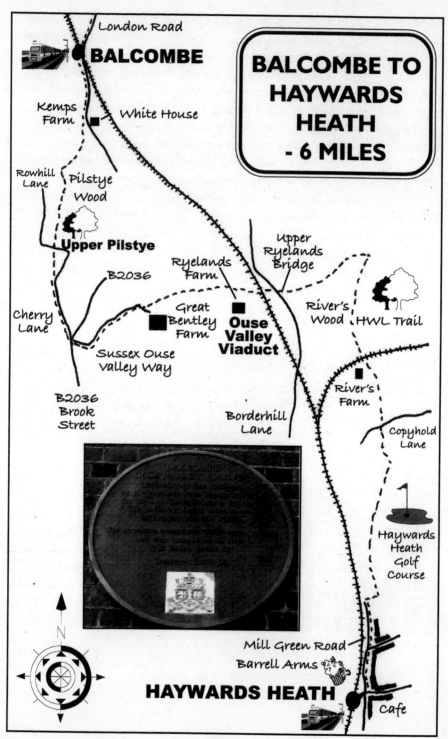

London Road

BALCOMBE

BALCOMBE TO HAYWARDS HEATH - 6 MILES

Kemps Farm

White House

Rowhill Lane

Pilstye Wood

Upper Pilstye

B2036

Ryelands Farm

Upper Ryelands Bridge

Cherry Lane

Great Bentley Farm

Ouse Valley Viaduct

River's Wood

HWL Trail

Sussex Ouse Valley Way

B2036 Brook Street

Borderhill Lane

River's Farm

Copyhold Lane

Haywards Heath Golf Course

N

Mill Green Road

Barrell Arms

HAYWARDS HEATH

Cafe

Stage Three

BALCOMBE TO HAYWARDS HEATH
- 6 MILES
- allow 2 1/2 hours
- 11,576 steps

Basic route - Balcombe - Kemps Farm - Pilstye Farm - Upper Pilstye - Cherry Lane - Sussex Ouse Valley Way - Great Bentley Farm - Ryelands Farm - Great Ouse Railway Viaduct - Borderhill Lane - Upper Ryelands Bridge - Rivers Wood - HWL Trail - River's Farm - Copyhold Lane - Highgrove Barn - Haywards Heath Golf Course - Wickham Farm - Mill Green Road - Haywards Heath & Station.

Map - O.S. Explorer 1:25,000 Series No - 135 - Ashdown Forest.

Start - Balcombe Station (GR. 306302).
End - Haywards Heath Station.

Inn - Burrell Arms, Haywards Heath.

Cafe - Haywards Heath.

ABOUT THE STAGE - A mixture of woodland and quiet countryside with no amenities until Haywards Heath, as you follow well defined paths. The climax of the stage is the Ouse Valley Railway Viaduct, an impressive piece of railway workmanship.

WALKING INSTRUCTIONS - Cross Balcombe Station via the footbridge to Platform 1 and exit into the car park. Turn left through the car park to the road - B2036. Turn right and follow the road right, with care, for 1/4 mile to Kemps Farm and prominent white house on the left. Turn right, as path signed, to a stile and then left to another and onto a path sign. Bear half right and

23

cross the field, descending slightly to a kissing gate and footbridge and enter Pilstye Wood. Ascend the path to another path sign and bear left passing on the right a rare exposed sandstone outcrop with the spectacular roots of a tree entwined - like a human - *see photo on left.* You are now following a track, leaving the wood keep a hedge on your right along level ground to the cluster of houses on the right - Upper Pilstye. Keep ahead to a stile, steps and path sign. Keep ahead to two stiles and continue along the edge of the field to a road - Rowhill Lane; to your left is Pilstye Farm.

Go straight across to a stile and steps and continue with the hedge on your right to the road - Cherry Lane. Bear right along it, ascending slightly and passing on your right, Hillside and Sidney Cottages. In little over 1/4 mile reach a road junction - B2036. Cross to your left to the farm drive of Great Bentley Farm (now heading eastwards) - footpath signed and part of the Sussex Ouse Valley Way. The drive swings left and in 1/4 mile turns sharp right to the farm. Here on the corner keep ahead, as path signed to a gate and steps. Continue with the hedge on your right to a footbridge - *see photo above* - and cross the next field passing a solitary oak tree on your right to a stile and path sign. Ascend up the field to the far righthand corner and two stiles as you pass

Ryelands Farm. The farm road turns left and you keep ahead to a stile and slowly descend the field to two stiles and pass under the Ouse Valley Viaduct.

SUSSEX OUSE VALLEY WAY - Opened in 2005, the 42 mile route, follows the River Ouse from it source near Lower Beeding, in the High Weald, to the sea at Sleaford Bay. The walks logo is the Ouse Valley Viaduct.

OUSE VALLEY RAILWAY VIADUCT - Designed by David Mocatta to carry the London - Brighton railway. Built in 1839-41, it rises 100 feet (30m) and is 500 yards long, with 37 arches, with balustrades and pavilions at either end. More than 11 million Dutch bricks were used in its construction; total cost - £38,500. Grade 2 listed building and an average of 110 trains cross the viaduct daily.

Ouse Valley Railway Viaduct - view through the arches showing some of the 11 million bricks!

Descend the field to Borderhill Lane and stile; you have fine views back to the viaduct from here. Turn right passing Wharf Cottages and cross the Upper Ryelands Bridge and immediately turn left, as path signed and stiled. Keep the stream on your left and you follow the path with woodland to your right. In 1/4 mile the path becomes a track as the wood joins you on the right. Entering a field can be seen two bridges ahead. Don't cross any; turn right, now heading southwards, to a stile and path sign, and enter River's Wood. Follow the defined path/track and in less 1/4 mile cross a track and keep ahead following the path signs marked - HWLT

HWLT - High Weald Landscape Trail - 90 miles (140 km) long between Horsham, West Sussex to Rye, East Sussex, passing through the High Weald Area of Outstanding Natural Beauty (AONB).

Continue to River's Road, and keep ahead across the branch railway line via the road bridge and pass River's Farm. Continue ahead to a footbridge and past woodland on the right to River's Farm Cottage. Keep ahead to Copyhold Lane. Here the HWLT turn right. Cross, as footpath signed to a kissing gate and follow the path to Highgrove Barn and Haywards Heath Golf Course. Turn right, as path signed, and follow the path past greens and fairways for more than 1/2 mile to the edge of Haywards Heath to Wickham Way and Wickham Farm. Turn right and shortly left along Mill Green Road to the centre of the town with Haywards Heath Rail Station on the right and Burrell Arms. There is a cafe on the left in the shop area.

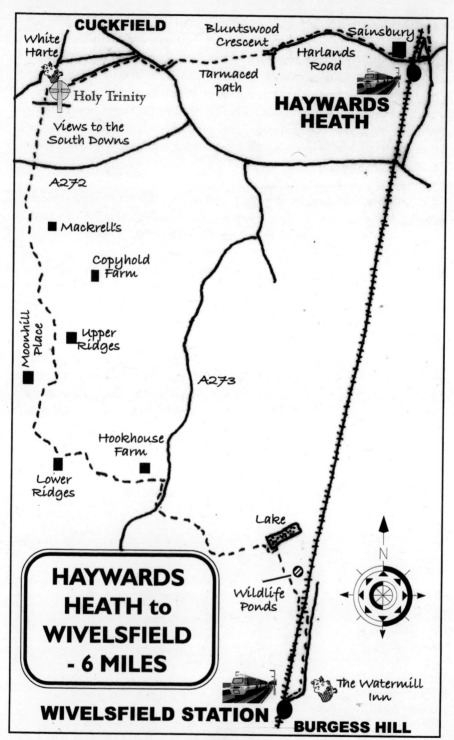

CUCKFIELD

White Harte

Holy Trinity

Views to the South Downs

A272

Bluntswood Crescent

Tarmaced path

Harlands Road

Sainsbury

HAYWARDS HEATH

Mackrell's

Copyhold Farm

Moonhill Place

Upper Ridges

A273

Hookhouse Farm

Lower Ridges

Lake

HAYWARDS HEATH to WIVELSFIELD - 6 MILES

Wildlife Ponds

N

WIVELSFIELD STATION

The Watermill Inn

BURGESS HILL

28

Stage Four

HAYWARDS HEATH to WIVELSFIELD STATION
- 6 MILES
- allow 2 1/2 hours.
- 12,690 steps.

Basic route - Haywards Heath (Station) - Harlands Road - Blunts Wood - Paiges Wood - Cuckfield - Holy Trinity church - A272 - Mackerell's - Old Furnace Cottage - Upper Ridges - Lower Ridges - A273 - Wivelsfield Station.

Map - O.S. 1:25,000 Explorer Series No. 135 - Ashdown Forest.

Start - Haywards Heath Station - GR 330246.
End - Wivelsfield Station.

Inns - Wheatsheaf Inn as you enter Cuckfield and the White Harte, just off the route near the church in Cuckfield. The Watermill Inn, Wivelsfield.

ABOUT THE STAGE - Pleasant walking on paths and tracks, across fields and past woodland. First you head westwards to Cuckfield and its imposing church, then south and eastwards to Wivelsfield. You have fine views to the South Downs, from Cuckfield onwards, the hilly bastion before Brighton!

WALKING INSTRUCTIONS - With your back to the station, turn left along Bannister Way, passing under the railway bridge and Sainsbury's on the right. Where the road turn sharp left, keep right along Harlands Road. Keep on this road for more than 1/2 mile to where it turns sharp left. Turn right along Blunts Wood Crescent. At the end turn left and right to walk through

Blunts Wood on a tarmaced path. Follow the path past Paige's Wood on the right and onto Hatchgate Lane, keeping ahead to the B2184 road in Cuckfield, almost opposite the Wheatsheaf Inn. Turn right and take the second road on your left - Courtmead Road (Private, but a right of way). Follow it to its end and on into the churchyard of Holy Trinity church. Keep ahead to the far side of the church and turn left along the path. Where you turn left just ahead is the White Harte Inn, in Cuckfield.

HOLY TRINITY CHURCH - Anglican. Dates from Norman times, but the present building is from the 13th. century onwards. Extended in the 14th. century with much restoration in Victorian times by Charles Eamer Kempe with stained glass by Kempe. The tub font is 13th. century. The buttressed tower has a broach spire.

You are now heading south with views to the South Downs. Walk past the gravestones to a gate and track. Turn right and left to continue on a track past Court House Farm; now a path to a stile and the A272 road. Cross to two kissing gates and keep ahead by the fence on your left to another kissing gate with Southern Water - Wastewater Treatment plant on the left. Keep ahead to footbridge and bear half left to pass Mackerell's on the left. Join a track still keeping ahead and where it turns sharp right, keep ahead over a stile by a path sign, and follow the path past woodland on the left to Copyhold Lane. Continue ahead passing Old Furnace Cottage. Immediately leave the lane, as path signed at a kissing gate and steps. Cross to a stile and path sign and bear left past woodland on a defined path and pass Upper Ridges. Keep ahead, as path signed, now on a track, turning left and right at the end to continue around a wood with Moonhill Place to your right. Follow the path right and left past another wood to a kissing gate, footpath sign and hedged track.

Turn left along the track, now heading south-east, to Lower Ridges, Follow the track left then right through woodland, and left again to pass Hookhouse Farm. Continue along the concrete drive to the A273 road. Turn right passing Holmbush Cottages on the left and take the second signed path on the left. Continue to a stile and path sign and keep the hedge on your left and a slim pond on your left and approach two footbridges. Take the first one on your left and ascend briefly before following the defined path past woodland and ascend steps to a path junction and lake. Turn right along the path past the spillway and then left and soon right to continue by the hedge on your right. Turn left and right to continue and pass a wildlife pond. Just after, ascend and cross the field to the far lefthand corner and railway line. Cross with care and soon after reach a road. Turn right and follow this into Wivelsfield to the The Watermill Inn and Wivelsfield Station on the right. If you are thru hiking, you do not need to go all the way to station. 1/4 mile before turn left, as path signed to begin the route to Hassocks Station.

WIVELSFIELD - *The rail station was known as Keymer Junction until 1896. Brighton is 9.3 miles away but some 24 miles, on foot to get there; but you are well over halfway!*

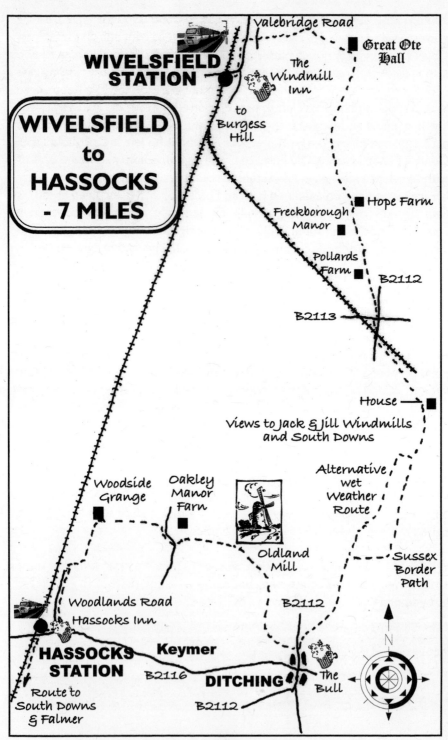

WIVELSFIELD STATION

Valebridge Road

Great Ote Hall

The Windmill Inn

to Burgess Hill

WIVELSFIELD to HASSOCKS - 7 MILES

Hope Farm

Freckborough Manor

Pollards Farm

B2112

B2113

House →

Views to Jack & Jill Windmills and South Downs

Alternative Wet Weather Route

Woodside Grange

Oakley Manor Farm

Oldland Mill

Sussex Border Path

Woodlands Road Hassocks Inn

B2112

Keymer

HASSOCKS STATION

B2116

DITCHING

The Bull

N

Route to South Downs & Falmer

B2112

Stage Five
WIVELSFIELD STATION to HASSOCKS STATION
- 7 MILES
- Allow 3 hours
- 13,695 steps

Basic Route - Wivelsfield Station - World's End - Great Ote Hall - Ote Hall Farm - Hope Farm - Freckborough Manor - Pollards Farm - B2113 - B2112 - Sussex Border Path - Ditchling - B2112 - Lodge Hill - Oldland Mill - Ockley Manor Farm - Woodside Grange - Woodsland Road - B2112 - Hassocks Station.

Map - O.S. 1:25,000 Explorer Series No. 122 - Brighton & Hove.

Start - Wivelsfield Station. GR. 323201.
End - Hassocks Station GR. 304156.

Inns - The Windmill Inn, near Wivelsfield Station. The Bull, Ditchling. Hassocks Inn near Hassocks Station.

ABOUT THE STAGE - Good walking along paths and tracks. First past Great Ote Hall and onto the crossroads near Ditchling Common and the boundary of East and West Sussex. You soon have fine views to the South Downs and you can see the Jack and Jill windmills, which you ascend past on the next stage! You soon pick up a section of the Sussex Border Path - there is an alternative path here if this section is waterlogged - which you follow to the attractive village of Ditchling. Well worth a visit and an inn just off the route! Your route now loops around Keymer and passes Oldland Windmill, dating back to 1703, before following a tarmaced path and road into Hassocks and station, with an inn opposite.

WALKING INSTRUCTIONS - Exiting Wivelsfield Station turn right along the road, past shops, to the road junction beside The Windmill Inn - you are in the World's End area of Burgess Hill. Turn left along Valebridge Road, retracing your route from Haywards Heath. After less than 1/4 mile beside house No. 48, turn right, as path signed. Follow the path to a road and go straight across and now along a fenced path to the end of the houses and a stile. Bear half left across the field following the path to a footpath sign. Turn right and keep to the lefthand edge of the field, beside the hedge to a road and houses. Keep ahead and soon pass the entrance gates of Great Ote Hall, on your left. Just after, turn right along the drive and pass Ote Hall Farm on the left to a road.

GREAT OTE HALL - *The present building is mostly early 17th. century and now a popular wedding venue, set in attractive grounds. previous owners have been the Governor of the Bahamas; the Governor of the Leeward Islands and the Godman family owned the hall in 1537 and descendants live here today.*
www.greatotehall.co.uk

Go straight across, to a stile and path sign. Continue with the hedge on your left to a stile and onto a concrete footbridge. Keep ahead on the defined path to houses and bridlepath sign. Turn left on the path with houses on your right. Where the path forks keep right in trees to another path junction; here keep left, as bridlepath signed. Continue to Hope Farm and follow the farm drive left and in 200 metres, turn right before the main road, at a gate. Follow the defined path paralleling the road, soon passing Freckborough Manor well to your right. Cross the drive and continue on the path and cross the drive to Pollards Farm on the right. Soon after gain the B2113 road and the boundaries of East and West Sussex.

Cross to your right to a path sign and continue on the path through woodland to the railway bridge and B2112 road. Cross the bridge and turn left, as path signed. First along the lefthand side of the field near the railway. In 1/4 mile is railway bridge No. 661. From here you have fine views ahead and to your right to the South Downs and the prominent Jack and Jill windmills, which you will pass on the penultimate stage. Bear half right across the field with a house to your left, to a stile and lift bar, put here by the Monday Group Volunteers - you will use a lot of these stiles for the next couple of miles. You are now on the Sussex Border Path.

SUSSEX BORDER PATH - *Created in 1983 the route keeps close to the inland boundary of Sussex and is 150 miles long. Starts at Emsworth, Hants - GR. SU753055 and ends at Rye, E. Sussex - GR, TQ753055. The route includes Thorney Island - see my separate walk guide to Hayling Island and Thorney Island.*
www.sussexborderpath.co.uk

There are two paths (rights of way) here and I found the righthand path kept to drier ground. Follow it to another stile and path junction. The path to the right - drier one - heads to a nursery and then turns left, becoming a fenced path, passing a field with four reindeer in. All is well stiled and a defined path. In 3/4 mile it joins the Sussex Border Path, where you keep straight ahead. If following the border Path; again this is well stiled and defined. Both paths meet at a gate. Turn left, following the Border Path, and keep the fence on your left to a high gate and free range hens. Keep ahead along the fenced path to another high gate, with Four Fields Farm on the left. Just after turn right at a stile and cross the field to a stile and then right on the path to North End, Ditchling. Turn right to the main B2112 road. Opposite is Boddington Lane and your route, but first turn left to see the attractive houses of Ditchling and The Bull Inn.

DITCHLING - *Amy Sawyer 1863-1945, the artist and playwright lived here. Until 1989 there was an artist community established by Eric Gill and known as The Guild of St. Joseph and St. Dominic. The 16th. century Bull Inn is one of the oldest buildings in this attractive village. Monks stayed here and the London to Brighton coaches stopped here. Accommodation - www.thebullditchling.com*

Follow Boddington Lane, passing Ponds Cottages on the left. Follow the road/track past Lodge Hill Cottage and up Lodge Hill to a stile on the left. Cross and follow the path right with spectacular views of the South Downs and to Oldland Windmill.

View to the South Downs and the Jack and Jill windmills on the righthand skyline; taken from near Oldland Windmill.

Follow the path to a ladder stile and then left by the fence to the windmill and drive. Bear left along it and in 1/4 mile left to a road on the edge of Keymer. Turn right and just around the corner turn left, opposite Ockley Manor, as path signed, along a track to Woodside Grange. Turn left and now on a tarmaced path head towards houses on the edge of Hassocks. Keep ahead on the wide path as it curves right to a road - Woodsland Road and railway line. Turn left along the road through Hassocks to the main road - B2116. Just before it, turn right to Hassocks Station and Hassocks Inn. The next stage is opposite the station.......and signed South Downs!

HASSOCKS - *As the name suggests the village is named after the tufts of grass found in the nearby fields. The London-Brighton railway with Hassocks Station built in 1841 developed village.*

OLDLAND WINDMILL - *Post mill dating back to 1703; sometimes known as Ditchling Windmill. Believed to be the only surviving post-mill in Southern England with a steam engine inside to grind corn on windless days. Being restored.*
www,oldlandmill.co.uk

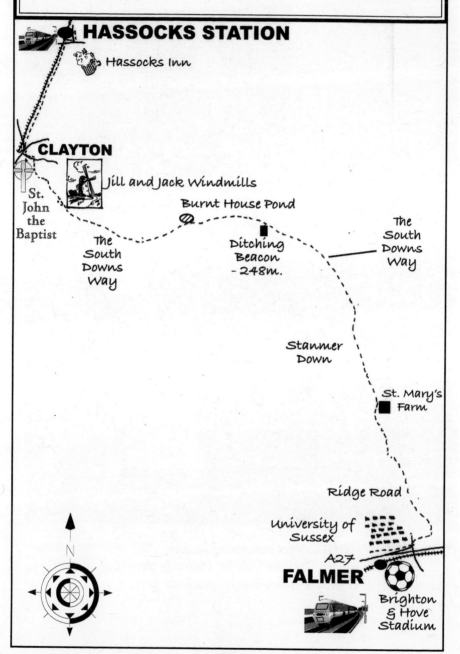

HASSOCKS to FALMER - 7 1/2 MILES

HASSOCKS STATION

Hassocks Inn

CLAYTON

Jill and Jack Windmills

St. John the Baptist

Burnt House Pond

The South Downs Way

Ditching Beacon - 248m.

The South Downs Way

Stanmer Down

St. Mary's Farm

Ridge Road

University of Sussex

A27

FALMER

Brighton & Hove Stadium

N

Stage Six –

HASSOCKS STATION TO FALMER STATION
- 7 1/2 MILES
- allow 3 hours
- 15,562 steps.

Basic Route - Hassocks Station - Butchers Wood - Lag Wood - Clayton - St. John the Baptist Church - Jill and Jack Windmills - South Downs Way - Ditching Beacon 248m. - Stanmer Down - St. Mary's Farm - Ridge Road - University of Sussex - Falmer Station.

Map - O.S. 1:25,000 Explorer Series No. 122 - Brighton & Hove.

Start - Hassocks Station GR. 304156.
End - Falmer Station GR. 347087

Inns - Hassocks Inn, Hassocks.

ABOUT THE STAGE - You have now arrived at the major highlight of the route - the effort has been worth it - as you ascend into the South Downs with spectacular views all around. First you walk to Clayton and its Norman church with medieval paintings. Then the ascent begins to the Jill and Jack Windmills and onto the South Downs Way. You reach Ditchling Beacon 248m. the highest point of the walk and views to the shining sea! You descend to St. Mary's Farm and ascend and descend to the University of Sussex and to Falmer Station. If you are continuing on, you do not need to go all the way to station, but turn left a mile before to continue along the final stage.

WALKING INSTRUCTIONS - Descend from the Station to the main road - B2116 - near the railway bridge - path opposite Hassocks Inn. Cross the road to a path sign - South Downs. Follow the straight tarmaced path beside

39

the railway line for nearly 1 1/2 miles. Pass Butchers Wood then Lag Wood and onto the road close to the Clayton Railway Tunnel. Turn left - footpath signed - South Downs 1 mile (Hassocks 1 1/2 miles). Take the second road on your left - Underhill Lane into Clayton village and pass St. John the Baptist church. Just before then you will have seen your first roadsign for Brighton!

CLAYTON TUNNEL - *Begun in 1839 and cost £90,000 for the 1 1/4 mile long tunnel, the second longest on the London-Brighton line. Lies 270 feet below ground and has an impressive castle keep like entrance, as seen from the footpath as you approach Clayton.*

ST. JOHN THE BAPTIST CHURCH, CLAYTON - *As is usual in the remotest corners of Britain you find a gem. Dating from Saxon times this simple church has walls covered in 12th. century wall paintings, which were "discovered" 700 years later. A visit is a must before ascending into the South Downs. The gate had a Domesday Plaque.*

Continue on along the lane following right and left and opposite Faversham house, turn right, as path - South Downs Way 3/4 mile. Ascend the path/track to a gate and turn left and soon right as you ascend the downs on a path to Jill Windmill and car park.

JACK AND JILL WINDMILLS - *Jill Windmill (post mill) - the first one you come too, has been restored; a 19th century corn mill. Built in 1821 in Brighton and known as Lashmar's New Mill on Dyke Road. It was brought here by a team of horses and oxen in 1852. Operated until 1906. Today it is open on Sundays - May to September. www.jillwindmill.org.uk*

Jack, a five story tower mill dates from 1866 and both Jill and Jack were working until 1906/7. Usually mills are considered female but this one is named a male - Jack.

Behind you are magnificent views back along your route and to Outlands Windmill. Before the car park turn left - path signed South Downs Way 1/4 mile. Walk past Jill and Jack windmills, turning right to a track. Turn left and shortly left again onto another track, now following the South Downs Way - Ditching Beacon 2 miles. In 3/4 mile at spot height 234m. beside the gate is a South Downs Marker showing Winchester and Eastbourne and to the right, Brighton!

SOUTH DOWNS WAY - *National Trail - 100 miles from Winchester to Eastbourne and the first dedicated bridlepath trail.*
www.southdownsway.co.uk

Keep ahead on the track along the high ground and pass Burnt House Pond on the left. Continue on the undulating grassy path and in 3/4 mile reach the trig point on the summit of Ditchling Beacon on the right. keeping ahead to Ditchling Road and car park - Ice Cream Van here in season.

The path towards Ditchling Beacon.

DITCHLING BEACON 248M - *Highest point in East Sussex and the third highest on the South Downs Way. National Trust property with 360 degree views. As the name suggests a warning beacon was lit here when invasion seemed imminent.*

View from Downs to Ditchling and Oldland Windmill - (Stage five.)

Cross to a gate and continue along the South Downs Way for a further 1/4 mile to a prominent grass track going across the down on the right. To reach it turn right and then left to a gate. Follow the gently descending path to a gate 1/2 mile away. Cross a shallow valley and ascend to a gate. Keep ahead on the path, soon with a hedge on your left and then a fence as you descend Stanmore Down to St. Mary's Farm. You will have seen in the distance the prominent stadium and University of Sussex - this is where Falmer station is!

Go through the gate and turn right past the farm of the drive/road and ascend past woodland and just after the road levels off there is a bridlepath, and small parking area, on the left - the final stage! If pressing on to Falmer Station continue along the road - Ridge Road - which in 1/2 mile upon reaching the outskirts of Falmer village, turn right along Mill Street. At the end turn left and right to descend the tarmaced cycle route close to the A27 slip road on the left. Turn left at the end to the underpass to Falmer Station, turning left to the station. You will retrace this mile long route at the start of the final stage, if starting from Falmer Station.

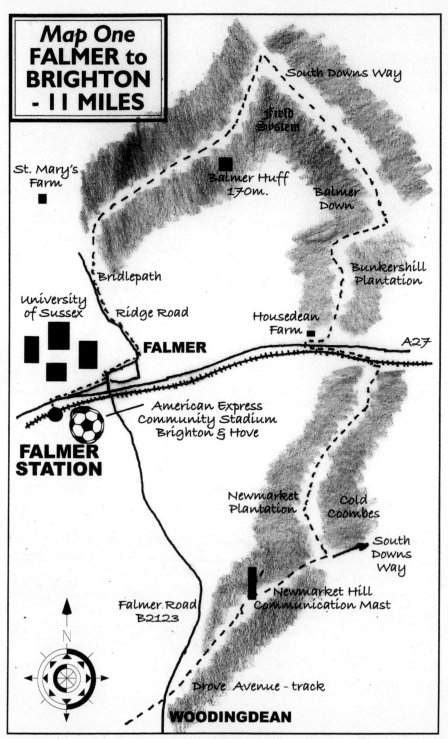

Map One
FALMER to
BRIGHTON
- 11 MILES

South Downs Way

Field
System

St. Mary's
Farm

Balmer Huff
170m.

Balmer
Down

Bunkershill
Plantation

Bridlepath

University
of Sussex

Ridge Road

Housedean
Farm

A27

FALMER

American Express
Community Stadium
Brighton & Hove

FALMER
STATION

Newmarket
Plantation

Cold
Coombes

South
Downs
Way

Newmarket Hill
Communication Mast

Falmer Road
B2123

N

Drove Avenue - track

WOODINGDEAN

44

Stage Seven

FALMER STATION to BRIGHTON PIER AND RAIL STATION
- 11 MILES
- allow 4 to 5 hours.
- 23, 839 steps (897 calories)

Basic route - Falmer Station - Falmer - Ridge Road - Balmer Huff - Buckland Bank - South Downs Way - Housedean Farm - A27 - South Downs Way - Newmarket Plantation - Newmarket Hill - Drove Avenue - Falmer Road (B2123) - Woodingdean - Drove Road - Sheepcote Valley Car park - Brighton Racecourse - East Brighton Golf Course - Red Hill - B2066 - Kemp Town - Black Rock Station - Volks Electric Railway - Brighton Pier - Brighton Rail Station.

Map - O.S. 1:25,000 Explorer Series No. 122 - Brighton & Hove.

START - Falmer Station.
END - Brighton Station.

Inns - Nothing until Brighton, which has everything. Drinking water tap at Housedean Farm beside the A27 - approx. halfway.

ABOUT THE STAGE - The last and longest one of the walk, but a glorious one! First you ascend back onto the South Downs and join the South Downs Way and descend to the A27. This is followed by a short gentle ascent to Newmarket Plantation, where soon after you leave the way. Crossing Newmarket Hill with views to Brighton, you pass Woodingdean to Brighton Racecourse, and begin the descent to Black Rock and Brighton Beach. Following near the shore and passing the shielded Naturalist area, you keep close to the Volks Electric Railway line to Brighton Pier. You continue a little further along the coast before turning right to reach Brighton Station. Near the pier you are close to the famous Royal Pavilion and well worth a side visit to see. You can also wander through the shopping area and lanes to the station. All in all a worthy end to a fascinating and varied walk from the outskirts of London to the shining sea.

WALKING INSTRUCTIONS - From Falmer Station entrance turn half left to the A27 underpass. The other side soon turn right onto a tarmaced path - a cycle route, signposted to Lewes. Follow the path right and left and beside the A27 slip road to the road junction and Falmer village. Turn left and right along Mill Street, passing Swan Cottages on the right and Pelham Cottages on the left. Reaching a road junction turn left along Ridge Road - a single lane road - retracing your steps past the Falmer Sports Complex on the left to where the road turns left. Here is a small parking area and bridlepath sign on the right. Follow this path, gently ascending, soon with views to your left down to St. Mary's Farm which you passed on the last stage. In 1/4 mile keep to high ground fenced path as you still slightly ascend to pass Balmer Huff 170m on the right. Passing through gates in 1/2 mile soon join a track along Buckland Bank and pass under electric pylons to the junction of the South Downs Way.

Turn right following track and again pass under the electricity wires, keeping a fence on your right as you start descending to a gate. Keep ahead descending to a stile, but don't cross, turn right to continue on the South Downs Way, descending towards Bunkershill Plantation. Enter the wood and follow the path uphill to the shoulder of Long Hill and gate. Keep ahead and follow the path downhill towards the A27 and tarmaced lane. Turn right and pass Housedean Farm (campsite) with a drinkable water tap in the wall - shut off in winter to avoid freezing up. Beyond the farm's entrance gates keep left uphill and turn left to cross the roadbridge over the A27. Follow the road left, downhill, and where it turns to join the A27, keep ahead to a gate and path beneath the railway line, on the right. In 1/4 mile turn right through Railway Bridge No. 710 to a gate and all the while still following the South Downs Way. You now begin a steady gentle ascent using gates and a hedge and fence with views left to Cold Coombes. Near the top with Newmarket Plantation on the right, turn left to continue on the defined South Downs Way to two gates. You have fine views eastwards from here to Newhaven. Reaching a track junction the South Downs Way turns left; here you leave it and turn right to follow the track to Newmarket Hill and prominent Communication Mast. On the way on the left is castle Hill Nature Reserve.

View down the path from near Newmarket Plantation.

Walk past the mast and where views to Brighton unfold, as you follow the track - Drove Avenue to a carpark and Falmer Road - B2123 - on the edge of Woodingdean, with Castle House on the left. Cross the road, as bridlepath signed and keep ahead along the track, now Drove Road. On your left are the houses of Woodingdean and to the right, below, Upper Bexendean. Keep straight ahead along the track for 3/4 miles to beyond the houses on the left to a road. Turn left along the path on the left following it round to Sheepcote Valley car park near a bus stop, on the right. Turn right to a kissing gate and cross the Brighton Racecourse and turn left on the defined path. First paralleling the course and then the East Brighton Golf Course on the left. Below to your right is Sheepcote Valley and Brighton! In almost a mile you near **Red Hill** 107m. and keep right as you descend the path/track to the golf Club House. Continue down the drive to the B2066 road.

Turn left and soon right along Cliff Approach - No Through Road. At the end keep ahead on a path along the righthand side of the field to steps down to the A259 road opposite Asda - over the wall - and Brighton Marina. Cross and turn right and soon left down the switch back path to Brighton Beach and Black Rock Station. On the left is the Naturalist Area. Turn right along the path near the railway with Brighton Pier ahead. Keep near the Volks Electric

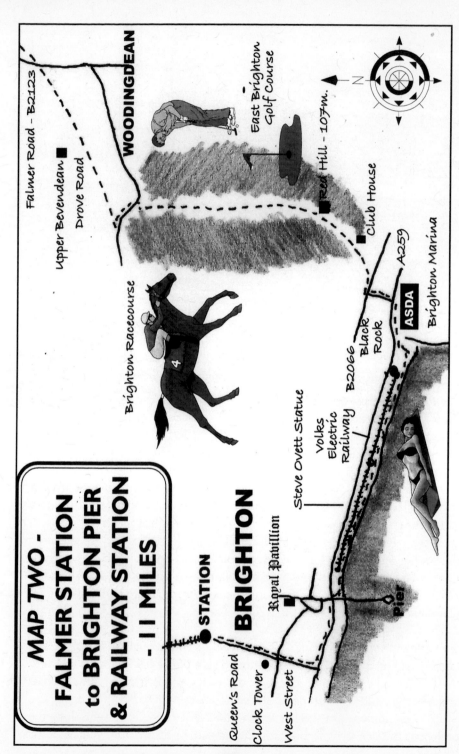

Railway line and walk towards the pier, passing a monument and statue to the legendary Olympian runner, Steve Ovett and the Brighton Wheel.

VOLKS ELECTRIC RAILWAY - *Opened on August 4th. 1883 by Magnus Volk and is today the world's oldest operating electric railroad. A mile long from the Aquarium near Brighton Pier to Black Rock near the marina. Open from March to September.*
www.volkselectricrailway.co.uk

Opposite the pier if you turn right past the Royal Albion Hotel and then left to the main shopping area with the Royal Pavilion a little further ahead. Those going to Brighton Station continue beside the sea along Grand Junction Road to West Street on the right. Turn right and keep ahead along it past the Clock Tower and on along Queen's Street to the station.

STEVE OVETT - *Being a mile runner he was and is one of my hero's! Born in Brighton hence his statue and monument recording his "Freedom of the City". An Olympian and world record holder for the 1500 metres and mile. He still holds the UK record for 2 miles set in 1978.*

Brighton Wheel and beach.

Brighton Pier entrance.

The Royal Pavilion, Brighton.

BRIGHTON - *More than a day can be spent exploring the variety of life found here, the shops, beach and historical landmarks.*
Royal Pavilion - once a royal palace built for the Prince Regent in the early 19th. century' designed by John Nash.
Brighton Pier - opened in 1899.
Brighton Wheel - opened in October 2011.
Clock tower - built to celebrate Queen Victoria's jubilee in 1888.

Congratulations

Sample completion certificate.

This is to certify that -
....
has walked 53 miles,
from Horley Station to Brighton Pier,
"from the outskirts of London to the sea",
by crossing the South Downs, river valleys, woodland
and villages in the area
to complete the
THE
BRIGHTON WAY
Happy walking
John N Merrill
THE JOHN MERRILL FOUNDATION
THE BRIGHTON WAY

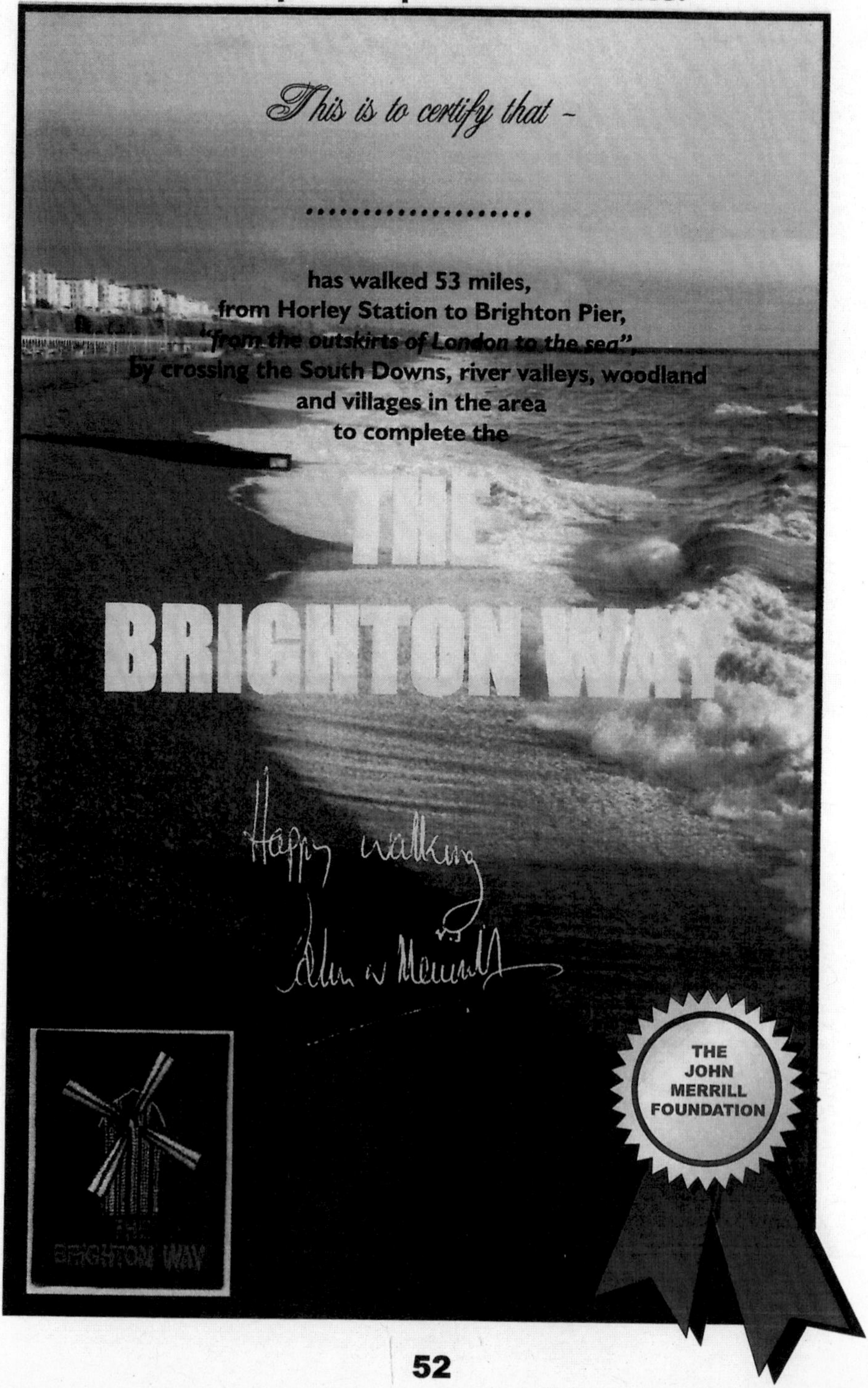

WALK
RECORD PAGE

Date walked -

Horley Station to Three Bridges Station - 8 1/2 miles ....

Three Bridges Station to Balcombe Station - 7 1/2 miles ....

Balcombe Station to Haywards Heath Station - 6 miles ....

Haywards Heath Station to Wivelsfield Station - 6 miles ....

Wivelsfield Station to Hassocks Station - 7 miles ....

Hassocks Station to Falmer Station - 7 1/2 miles ....

Falmer Station to Brighton Station - 11 miles ....

THE BRIGHTON WAY WALK BADGE

Complete the walk in this book and get the special embroidered badge opposite, and signed certificate. Badges are blue cloth with lettering and windmill embroidered in four colours.

BADGE ORDER FORM

Date walks completed...

NAME ....

ADDRESS ....

....

Price: £6.00 each including postage, packing, VAT and signed completion certificate. Amount enclosed (Payable to The John Merrill Foundation) ..
From: The John Merrill Foundation,
32, Holmesdale, Waltham Cross, Hertfordshire. EN8 8QY

Tel/Fax 01992 - 762776
e-mail - marathonhiker@aol.com
www.johnmerrillwalkguides.co.uk

THE JOHN MERRILL TWO CHALLENGE WALK AND FOUR CHALLENGE WALK BADGES - Complete two or four of John Merrill Challenge Walks and get a yellow (two challenge) or red (four challenge badge) and a special signed certificate.

OTHER BOOKS by Revd. John N. Merrill

CIRCULAR WALK GUIDES -

SHORT CIRCULAR WALKS IN THE PEAK DISTRICT - Vols. 1 to 9
CIRCULAR WALKS IN WESTERN PEAKLAND
SHORT CIRCULAR WALKS IN THE STAFFORDSHIRE MOORLANDS
SHORT CIRCULAR WALKS - TOWNS & VILLAGES OF THE PEAK DISTRICT
SHORT CIRCULAR WALKS AROUND MATLOCK
SHORT CIRCULAR WALKS IN "PEAK PRACTICE COUNTRY."
SHORT CIRCULAR WALKS IN THE DUKERIES
SHORT CIRCULAR WALKS IN SOUTH YORKSHIRE
SHORT CIRCULAR WALKS IN SOUTH DERBYSHIRE
SHORT CIRCULAR WALKS AROUND BUXTON
SHORT CIRCULAR WALKS AROUND WIRKSWORTH
SHORT CIRCULAR WALKS IN THE HOPE VALLEY
40 SHORT CIRCULAR WALKS IN THE PEAK DISTRICT
CIRCULAR WALKS ON KINDER & BLEAKLOW
SHORT CIRCULAR WALKS IN SOUTH NOTTINGHAMSHIRE
SHORT CIRCULAR WALKS IN CHESHIRE
SHORT CIRCULAR WALKS IN WEST YORKSHIRE
WHITE PEAK DISTRICT AIRCRAFT WRECKS
CIRCULAR WALKS IN THE DERBYSHIRE DALES
SHORT CIRCULAR WALKS FROM BAKEWELL
SHORT CIRCULAR WALKS IN LATHKILL DALE
CIRCULAR WALKS IN THE WHITE PEAK
SHORT CIRCULAR WALKS IN EAST DEVON
SHORT CIRCULAR WALKS AROUND HARROGATE
SHORT CIRCULAR WALKS IN CHARNWOOD FOREST
SHORT CIRCULAR WALKS AROUND CHESTERFIELD
SHORT CIRCULAR WALKS IN THE YORKS DALES - Vol 1 - Southern area.
SHORT CIRCULAR WALKS IN THE AMBER VALLEY (Derbyshire)
SHORT CIRCULAR WALKS IN THE LAKE DISTRICT
SHORT CIRCULAR WALKS IN THE NORTH YORKSHIRE MOORS
SHORT CIRCULAR WALKS IN EAST STAFFORDSHIRE
LONG CIRCULAR WALKS IN THE PEAK DISTRICT - Vol.1 to 5.
DARK PEAK AIRCRAFT WRECK WALKS
LONG CIRCULAR WALKS IN THE STAFFORDSHIRE MOORLANDS
LONG CIRCULAR WALKS IN CHESHIRE
WALKING THE TISSINGTON TRAIL
WALKING THE HIGH PEAK TRAIL
WALKING THE MONSAL TRAIL & SETT VALLEY TRAILS
PEAK DISTRICT WALKING - TEN "TEN MILER'S" - Vol 1 and 2.
CLIMB THE PEAKS OF THE PEAK DISTRICT
PEAK DISTRICT WALK A MONTH Vols One, Two, Three, Four, Five & Six
TRAIN TO WALK Vol. One - The Hope Valley Line
DERBYSHIRE LOST VILLAGE WALKS -Vol One and Two.
CIRCULAR WALKS IN DOVEDALE AND THE MANIFOLD VALLEY
CIRCULAR WALKS AROUND GLOSSOP
WALKING THE LONGDENDALE TRAIL
WALKING THE UPPER DON TRAIL
SHORT CIRCULAR WALKS IN CANNOCK CHASE
CIRCULAR WALKS IN THE DERWENT VALLEY
WALKING THE TRAILS OF NORTH-EAST DERBYSHIRE
WALKING THE PENNINE BRIDLEWAY & CIRCULAR WALKS
SHORT CIRCULAR WALKS ON THE NEW RIVER & SOUTH-EAST HERTFORDSHIRE
SHORT CIRCULAR WALKS IN EPPING FOREST

WALKING THE STREETS OF LONDON
LONG CIRCULAR WALKS IN EASTERN HERTFORDSHIRE
LONG CIRCULAR WALKS IN WESTERN HERTFORDSHIRE
WALKS IN THE LONDON BOROUGH OF ENFIELD
WALKS IN THE LONDON BOROUGH OF BARNET
WALKS IN THE LONDON BOROUGH OF HARINGEY
WALK IN THE LONDON BOROUGH OF WALTHAM FOREST
SHORT CIRCULAR WALKS AROUND HERTFORD
THE BIG WALKS OF LONDON
SHORT CIRCULAR WALKS AROUND BISHOP'S STORTFORD
SHORT CIRCULAR WALKS AROUND EPPING DISTRICT
CIRCULAR WALKS IN THE BOROUGH OF BROXBOURNE
LONDON INTERFAITH WALKS - Vol 1 and Vol. 2
LONG CIRCULAR WALKS IN THE NORTH CHILTERNS
SHORT CIRCULAR WALKS IN EASTERN HERTFORDSHIRE
WORCESTERSHIRE VILLAGE WALKS by Des Wright
WARWICKSHIRE VILLAGE WALKS by Des Wright
WALKING AROUND THE ROYAL PARKS OF LONDON
WALKS IN THE LONDON BOROUGH OF CHELSEA AND ROYAL KENSINGTON

CANAL WALKS -

VOL 1 - DERBYSHIRE & NOTTINGHAMSHIRE
VOL 2 - CHESHIRE & STAFFORDSHIRE
VOL 3 - STAFFORDSHIRE
VOL 4 - THE CHESHIRE RING
VOL 5 - THE GRANTHAM CANAL
VOL 6 - SOUTH YORKSHIRE
VOL 7 - THE TRENT & MERSEY CANAL
VOL 8 - WALKING THE DERBY CANAL RING
VOL 9 - WALKING THE LLANGOLLEN CANAL
VOL 10 - CIRCULAR WALKS ON THE CHESTERFIELD CANAL
VOL 11 - CIRCULAR WALKS ON THE CROMFORD CANAL
Vol.13 - SHORT CIRCULAR WALKS ON THE RIVER LEE NAVIGATION -Vol. 1 - North
Vol. 14 - SHORT CIRCULAR WALKS ON THE RIVER STORT NAVIGATION
Vol.15 - SHORT CIRCULAR WALKS ON THE RIVER LEE NAVIGATION - Vol. 2 - South
Vol. 16 - WALKING THE CANALS OF LONDON
Vol 17 - WALKING THE RIVER LEE NAVIGATION
Vol. 20 - SHORT CIRCULAR WALKS IN THE COLNE VALLEY
Vol 21 - THE BLACKWATER & CHELMER NAVIGATION - End to End.
Vol. 22 - NOTTINGHAM'S LOST CANAL by Bernard Chell.
Vol. 23 - WALKING THE RIVER WEY & GODALMING NAVIAGTIONS END TO END
Vol.25 - WALKING THE GRAND UNION CANAL - LONDON TO BIRMINGHAM.

JOHN MERRILL DAY CHALLENGE WALKS

WHITE PEAK CHALLENGE WALK
THE HAPPY HIKER - WHITE PEAK - CHALLENGE WALK
DARK PEAK CHALLENGE WALK
PEAK DISTRICT END TO END WALKS
STAFFORDSHIRE MOORLANDS CHALLENGE WALK

JOHN MERRILL DAY CHALLENGE WALKS

WHITE PEAK CHALLENGE WALK
THE HAPPY HIKER - WHITE PEAK - CHALLENGE WALK No.2
DARK PEAK CHALLENGE WALK
PEAK DISTRICT END TO END WALKS
STAFFORDSHIRE MOORLANDS CHALLENGE WALK
THE LITTLE JOHN CHALLENGE WALK
YORKSHIRE DALES CHALLENGE WALK
NORTH YORKSHIRE MOORS CHALLENGE WALK
LAKELAND CHALLENGE WALK
THE RUTLAND WATER CHALLENGE WALK
MALVERN HILLS CHALLENGE WALK
THE SALTERIS WAY
THE SNOWDON CHALLENGE
CHARNWOOD FOREST CHALLENGE WALK
THREE COUNTIES CHALLENGE WALK (Peak District).
CAL-DER-WENT WALK
THE QUANTOCK WAY
BELVOIR WITCHES CHALLENGE WALK
THE CARNEDDAU CHALLENGE WALK
THE SWEET PEA CHALLENGE WALK
THE LINCOLNSHIRE WOLDS - BLACK DEATH - CHALLENGE WALK
JENNIFER'S CHALLENGE WALK
THE EPPING FOREST CHALLENGE WALK
THE THREE BOROUGH CHALLENGE WALK - NORTH LONDON
THE HERTFORD CHALLENGE WALK
THE BOSHAM CHALLENGE WALK
THE KING JOHN CHALLENGE WALK
THE NORFOLK BROADS CHALLENGE WALK
THE RIVER MIMRAM WALK
THE ISLE OF THANET CHHALENGE WALK

INSTRUCTION & RECORD -

HIKE TO BE FIT.....STROLLING WITH JOHN
THE JOHN MERRILL WALK RECORD BOOK
HIKE THE WORLD - John Merrill's guide to walking & Backpacking.

MULTIPLE DAY WALKS -

THE RIVERS'S WAY
PEAK DISTRICT: HIGH LEVEL ROUTE
PEAK DISTRICT MARATHONS
THE LIMEY WAY
THE PEAKLAND WAY
COMPO'S WAY by Alan Hiley
THE BRIGHTON WAY

COAST WALKS & NATIONAL TRAILS -

ISLE OF WIGHT COAST PATH
PEMBROKESHIRE COAST PATH
THE CLEVELAND WAY
WALKING ANGELSEY'S COASTLINE.
WALKING THE COASTLINE OF THE CHANNEL ISLANDS
THE ISLE OF MAN COASTAL PATH - "The Way of the Gull."
A WALK AROUND HAYLING ISLAND
A WALK AROUND THE ISLE OF SHEPPEY
A WALK AROUND THE ISLE OF JERSEY
WALKING AROUND THE ISLANDS OF ESSEX

DERBYSHIRE & PEAK DISTRICT HISTORICAL GUIDES -

A to Z GUIDE OF THE PEAK DISTRICT
DERBYSHIRE INNS - an A to Z guide
HALLS AND CASTLES OF THE PEAK DISTRICT & DERBYSHIRE
TOURING THE PEAK DISTRICT & DERBYSHIRE BY CAR
DERBYSHIRE FOLKLORE
PUNISHMENT IN DERBYSHIRE
CUSTOMS OF THE PEAK DISTRICT & DERBYSHIRE
WINSTER - a souvenir guide
ARKWRIGHT OF CROMFORD
LEGENDS OF DERBYSHIRE
DERBYSHIRE FACTS & RECORDS
TALES FROM THE MINES by Geoffrey Carr
PEAK DISTRICT PLACE NAMES by Martin Spray
DERBYSHIRE THROUGH THE AGES - Vol 1 -DERBYSHIRE IN PREHISTORIC TIMES
SIR JOSEPH PAXTON
FLORENCE NIGHTINGALE
JOHN SMEDLEY
BONNIE PRINCE CHARLIE & 20 mile walk.
THE STORY OF THE EARLS AND DUKES OF DEVONSHIRE

JOHN MERRILL'S MAJOR WALKS -

TURN RIGHT AT LAND'S END
WITH MUSTARD ON MY BACK
TURN RIGHT AT DEATH VALLEY
EMERALD COAST WALK
I CHOSE TO WALK - Why I walk etc.
A WALK IN OHIO - 1,310 miles around the Buckeye Trail.
I AM GUIDED - the story of John's life.

SKETCH BOOKS -

SKETCHES OF THE PEAK DISTRICT

COLOUR BOOK:-

THE PEAK DISTRICT.......something to remember her by.

OVERSEAS GUIDES -

HIKING IN NEW MEXICO - Vol I - The Sandia and Manzano Mountains.
Vol 2 - Hiking "Billy the Kid" Country.
Vol 4 - N.W. area - " Hiking Indian Country."
"WALKING IN DRACULA COUNTRY" - Romania.
WALKING THE TRAILS OF THE HONG KONG ISLANDS.

VISITOR GUIDES - MATLOCK . BAKEWELL. ASHBOURNE.

See all my books on -
www.johnmerrillwalkguides.co.uk

Pilgrim guides -
www.thejohnmerrillministry.co.uk

WALK THE NATIONAL FOREST WAY - 75 MILES

The author at the start.

In June 2017 I walked the National Forest Way from the National Monument Arboretum in Staffordshire to Beacon Hill in Charnwood Forest, Leicestershire.

It is a good walk through Staffordshire, South Derbyshire and in Leicestershire, following a mixture of paths and tracks. I camped where possible and Moira has both a Youth Hostel and campsite. You walk beside the Trent & Mersey Canal, through much woodland, past reservoirs and many historical buildings, including Calke Abbey. The final section is through Bradgate Park and onto the summit of Beacon Hill, a stunning climax. All in all an enjoyable 4 day walk in the Midlands.

www.nationalforestway.co.uk

A walker.

There is a walker
who in his youth walked
up hill and down dale.
As the years passed he
went for longer walks,
not 20 or 30 miles or
even 100 miles,
but walks of a minimum of
1,000 miles.
He progressed to 1,500 miles,
then 2,100 miles and knew
he was ready for the big one.
7,000 miles around Britain.
He then left these shores
and did long walks in
Europe, America and Asia.
So far has done more than
219,500 miles and written
450 books, while wearing
out 134 pairs of boots.
He has never been ill,
or broken a bone or been
in hospital.
He has had no new knees or
hips, he is in the same body
that he was born with.
Who is this man?
Why me, Revd. John Merrill!

May the sun bring you new energy by day.
May the moon softly restore you by night.
May the rain wash away your worries.
May the breeze blow new strength into your being.
May you walk gbently through the world and
Know its beauty all the days of your life.

Apache blessing.

Look at the trees.
Look at the birds.
Look at the clouds.
Look at the stars ……..
And if you have eyes
you will be able to see
that the whole of
existence is joyful.

Osho.

THE JOHN MERRILL MINISTRY
- a universal monk -
embracing & honouring
all faiths & none.

John has been following his own spiritual path all his life, and is guided. He was brought up as a Christian and confirmed at the age of 13. He then went to a Quaker Boarding School for five years and developed his love for the countryside and walking. He became fascinated with Tibet and whilst retaining his Christian roots, became immersed in Buddhism. For four years he studied at the Tara Buddhist Centre in Derbyshire. He progressed into Daoism and currently attends the Chinese Buddhist Temple (Pure Land Tradition) in London. With his thirst for knowledge and discovery he paid attention to other faiths and appreciated their values. Late in life he decided it was time to reveal his spiritual beliefs and practices and discovered the Interfaith Seminary.

'When the pupil is ready, the teacher will appear'. (Buddhist saying).

Here for two years he learnt in more depth the whole spectrum of faiths , including   Jainism, Paganism, Mother Earth, Buddhism, Hinduism, Islam, Judaism, Sikhism, Celtic Worship and Shamanism. This is an ongoing exploration without end. He embraces all faiths, for all have a beauty of their own. All paths/faiths lead to one goal/truth. On July 17th. 2010 he was Ordained as a Multi-faith Minister.

'May you go in peace, with joy in your heart
and may the divine be always at your side.'

Using his knowledge and experience he combines many faiths into a simple, caring and devoted services, individually made for each specific occasion, with dignity and honour.
He conducts special Ceremonies -

Popular Funeral Celebrant and member of the Natural Death Society.

* Funerals * Memorial Services * Sermons * Weddings   *Civil Partnerships
* Baby Blessings & Naming
* Rites of Passage * Healing Ceremonies * Pilgimages * Inspirational Talks
Qigong Teacher.   Reiki Prationer.

For further information Contact John on -
Tel/Fax: 01992 - 762776   Mobile. 07910 889429
Email - universalmonk@oulook.com
Ministry site -www.thejohnmerrillministry.co.uk
All Faiths church - www.londoninterfaithchurch.co.uk

Revd. John N. Merrill, HonMUni
32, Holmesdale, Waltham Cross,
Hertfordshire EN8 8QY